Messages to Federico

i.m. Federico Garcia Lorca (1898-1936)

Michael Glover

©Michael Glover 2018

Cover image copyright © Michael Glover
Cover font "Alegraya" copyright © 2011, Juan Pablo del Peral (juan@huertatipografica.com.ar),

ISBN 978-1-9996440-3-1

www.1889books.co.uk

Other poetry publications by Michael Glover:

Measured Lives (1994)
Impossible Horizons (1995)
A Small Modicum of Folly (1997)
The Bead-Eyed Man (1999)
Amidst All This Debris (2001)
For the Sheer Hell of Living (2009)
Only So Much (2011)
Hypothetical May Morning (2018)

For Jesse, Joseph and Ruth

Contents

A Message to Federico	1
Federico's Unexpected Departure	2
Not Leaving Me, Federico	3
I Caught You, Federico	4
The Taste of Federico	5
Death's Anonymity	6
The Miracle	7
Federico as the Hanging Moon	8
Jump, Federico!	9
Dealing-Death with Federico	10
How Could We Expect You to Know, Federico?	11
After Your Death, Federico	12
Wake up, Federico!	13
The Streets of Granada	14
The Plains of the Vega	15
The Tragic Loss of the Cicadas and the Butterflies	16
Return and Departure	17
Federico's Lightness of Step	18
Always this Lostness	19
The Lizard	20
Embracing the Wraith of Federico	21
The Calling Back	22
Was It Not You, Federico?	23
Night, Night	24
The Game of Patience	25
Star-Struck, Star-Crossed	26
Baahling Federico!	27
The Wind Grieves for Federico	28

Not Just Yet, Federico	29
Federico's Impatience	30
Believing in Federico	31
Setting Federico Free	32
Que raro que me llame Federico!	33
Federico's Whisperings	34
Together, Federico	35
It Is All Too Awful	36
Never To Know	37
An Unexpected Invitation to Paradise	38
A Prayer for Federico	39
Unpicking Death's Mystery	40
Death, There Is No Word For It	41
Death's Intimacy	42
The Cold Corridors	43
For All Eternity, Federico	44
Papa Death	45
Time Unmakes Its Favours, Federico…	46
All Of This May Be You	47
Swimming with Debussy	48
The Bottles	49
Since Your Death, Federico	50
My Death for Yours, Federico?	51
Federico Is Not Dead	52
This Endless Waiting	53
Questions for Federico	54
Federico Falls Away From Himself	55
Your Killers, Federico	56
You Will Be Transported, Federico	57
Broken	58

Federico is Not There	59
Often You Were Barely There,	
So Sunken Were You Inside Yourself	60
Federico, Fire Fly	61
Showing the Way	62
Fools, Fools	63
The Curiosity of the Universe	64
All	65

A Message to Federico

Whose hand is this
so close to the orchard?
Whose blood-stained hand
is still beckoning to me?

Whose face is this,
averted in anguish,
beneath the olive trees?
Surely these eyes are not closed
in death's sleep...

Not so, not so, Federico!
You leap into my arms again,
your young blood pulsing.
I hold you now for as long as I am able.
I hold you here forever, my Federico.

Federico's Unexpected Departure

You were borne away from here so quickly.
I did not have time to say my goodbyes to you.
By the time I arrived, you had already gone.
The cart was drawing away, throwing dust into my eyes.
And after the cart followed the harsh
        words of the sexton.

I am still looking for you everywhere
beneath the trees of this olive grove.
I see your handprints, your footprints.
There is nowhere that you are not.
There is nowhere you have not been seen to go.
Your smile is in this olive in my mouth.
Your gestures of pain as you fell
are in the hellish twisting of these limbs.

Not Leaving Me, Federico

You have not yet slipped out of my arms, Federico.
The warmth of you is still beside me.
Your words are being whispered in my ear.

The tamarind tree is rising up in my dreams.
I hear the fierce jangle of your music.
I even see you dancing in front of me.

Federico, your bow tie is a little askew this morning.
Let me adjust it for you. And, by the way,
You will hate these New York streets.

Step lightly then.
Do not let them burn
the soles of your lovely feet.

I Caught You, Federico

I caught you back
just when you were falling.
I said to you:
you are still that young tree
which is reaching towards its maturity.
Now is not the moment to leave us.

And so you hesitated in your falling,
and you looked at me
for as long as it took for
the bullet to pierce you.
That is how long it lasted, Federico,
your piercing look.

The Taste of Federico

Your taste was never bitter
as this after-life is bitter,
these long moments,
which will end
only when I see you.

And I am due, always, to see you
when I speak your words out loud
in the quiet of my heart.
Will you see me *then*,
which may be now?

Death's Anonymity

It is this that I pray:
Not exactly forever, Federico.
Not exactly forever
will you be gone from me.

Your footsteps were with me this morning.
You greeted me, lips pressed to my lips.
Do you not remember
all that you meant to me?

It was all a terrible hurrying away.
And I was not there to catch you.
All these days are the one day.

Now, when I turn to you,
you are forever turned away
in death's terrible anonymity.

The Miracle

They have bulldozed the very ground on which you fell.
They have removed every last inkling of you.
Your hair has ascended to the heavens.
Your bow tie is transformed into a butterfly.

Your eyes are minerals, buried deep in the earth,
····unreachable.
Your voice is one amongst the many voices of the wind.
And still I am feeling you here beside me.
Still I am clutching your hand.

You have granted me that miracle, Federico.

Federico as the Hanging Moon

You stepped so lightly.
And then you were gone.
Yours was the voice of the wind.

Granada has drawn a cloak about itself.
Granada is whispering to me
in the most hushed of hushed tones.

Where will it find you now?
Where have you hidden yourself?
Are you rock, mineral,
       the cicadas' agitations in the evening?

You are the hanging moon, Federico.
You are biding your time.

Jump, Federico!

I have counted the days of your death –
one, two, three
and a *jump* into the heavens!

Where did you learn such tricks?
Were you that tiny bird just then
poised on the end of a stick?

Now I sleep inside your voice.
I am lapped and lifted
by the long lullaby of your singing.

Yours was not a perfect voice, Federico.
Like you, it was not strong to resist
that evil which engulfed us in the end.

Dealing-Death with Federico

No, no, no, I said to you,
do not return to Granada.
There is a stench of evil
in the public wells.
The waters are poisoned.

You would not look back at me.
Your courage was yanking you
by the collar and saying:
come, come, Federico,
their guns and their mortars
are so much puppetry!

They will listen to
the protestations of your tender fingers
pulling at the strings.
The abyss that is riding the wind
is all an illusion,
as are the fool words themselves:
death-dealing.

How Could We Expect You to Know, Federico?

Your frenzy was too much for you.
You could not hold it all.
The vessel of your body was too flimsy.
You always breathed too quickly!

How could we expect you to know?
You were always at death's bidding.
He it was who wrote the greatest words
of your finest poetry.

How could we expect you to know?
You were a child – in spite of your appearance.
Your child's laughter still spills across these fields.
Your child's laughter is in this water in my mouth.

After Your Death, Federico

After your death, Federico,
I carried you back to the Vega.
It was not difficult for me.
You had become lighter than
a favoured pebble in a poacher's pocket.

In fact,
I danced you from hand to hand
as if you were a puppet
in your own puppet show,
manipulated by your own dear hand.
See! See how easy!

How you sang for me then!
How we laughed together!
How timeless that day seemed!
And how we swore to each other
to live together
in that dreamspace forever...

Wake up, Federico!

Federico, my friend, wake up,
wake up again,
wake up,
as on any other morning.

I cannot abide
for your body to be so still.
The redness around your mouth
is not an oozing of blood.

It is the redness of your passion
when we kiss again, again...
Wake up, Federico.
Try not to be so lazy.

I am not inclined to kick you awake.

The Streets of Granada

I have asked for space
to consider your death.
The space of a thousand acres.
The space of your life's short length.
The space of eternity.
Will that be sufficient?
I doubt it.

I will still be crowding in about you
asking you why why why,
and you will still be,
as you have always been,
standing nearby,
casually looking and talking,
always talking...

...and writing it out of yourself,
your ever unspooling story,
threading it, around and about,
through the streets of Granada.

The Plains of the Vega

When I think I may have said it all,
a little more is always forthcoming.
The stone tosses in a word.
The olive pip opens its mouth.
The inkwell thirsts.
A pencil fidgets.
Even your chair back
creaks in sympathy this morning.

And then there is all that you once saw
and will forever now be seeing
from this window...
The plains of the Vega,
spread so gorgeously today,
those arms still beckoning you,
ever more and more welcoming...

The Tragic Loss of the Cicadas and the Butterflies

The cicadas and the butterflies
have all gathered here again,
asking how to make amends
for your untimely passing.

They did not do enough to shield you.
You were their friend.
When they danced,
you danced with them.

When they fell silent
or closed their wings prayerfully,
you mimicked them
until they all laughed with you
in the brightest of bright sunshines.

What will they do now without you?
How can a butterfly, once so yellow,
ever ease off its grey-sky mourning garments
now that it knows for sure
that it has lost you?

Return and Departure

When morning returns again,
you return with it.
You are writing at your desk again.
We share the pleasures of each other's company.

As evening approaches,
I see how you are thinning
until I see through you to storm clouds,
men running, spasmodic shouting.

I catch at you as you leave me.
You are flailing your arms.
There is no singing.
All is now as it will forever be.

Federico's Lightness of Step

If only I possessed
your lightness of step, Federico,
I would not need to envy you.

I would step into your shoes
and sing and dance with you,
just the two of us together,

linked arms,
linked hearts,
linked destinies.

Your death has robbed me of myself
because I was already you
when you stared at me.

I entered into you. I absorbed you.
We became each other,
brothers, lovers, bodily and intangibly.

And now I am less than a half
of what I am.
I barely know myself in the mirror.

The little that I see
is all that you have left of me,
and it is you, you, you,
as it will always be,
my bodily brother,
my intangible lover.

Always this Lostness

Always this lostness
without Federico.
Too many spaces.
Too much time.
Too many voices jangling.
Too much purposeless crying.

Always this lostness
without Federico.
The cat has turned its back on me.
The pig wallows in its mud.
Six small singing birds
have taken their vows of silence.

Which one of you has remembered today?
Is the old man's pipe being smoked
for the bitterest of reasons?
Are you selling those oranges
as a gesture of homage?
Why so little news of his death?
Why such complicit silence?
Why have the heavens not snapped in two
like a sacramental wafer?

The Lizard

The sun-stunned lizard,
entirely motionless,
remembers nothing.
It says not one word back to me.

Why then, when I approach,
does it dart away so suddenly?
Is it you, Federico,
making your vain apologies?

Am I so much to be feared
that you need to leave me?

Embracing the Wraith of Federico

I was falling directly into your arms
when you did not catch me.
I was making a gesture of renunciation
as you were walking away from me.

When I explained my death to you,
you showed me a map
of the human heart,
with all its busy workings.

When I told you that
I would not and could not be with you,
you lifted the calendar from the wall,

with the long days tolling ahead of us.
But this is not me! I cried out to you,
jabbing at February, August, April.

These are all our months to come,
you said, smiling, as you tenderly
embraced the wraith of me.

The Calling Back

I asked us both to think
of the newness of it all –
how life gleams
when the morning sun bounces off it!

I asked us both to think
of the preciousness of it all –
your love for me
and mine for you.

We are this venerated casket
which moves ahead so slowly
in a holy procession
of mutual devotedness.

Is this not how it will be,
Federico? I ask you.
Is this not how it would have been?
destiny's grey voice calls back to me.

Was It Not You, Federico?

Federico, you firefly,
did I not see you just then
on this terrace beneath the moon
out of the corner of my eye?
Did you not wink, and were gone
as if you had never been,

as if I had imagined you here
beneath this moon,
on this terrace,
with the night deep-inked in,
and a flung sprinkle of stars
across my shoulder?
Was it not you again, Federico,
saying: oh, come, come?

Night, Night

Night, night again, Federico!
Too much of it

with no one
to reach for.

Is that your voice again calling?
It must be.

Let me hurry
as I lie here.

Let me hurry
to embrace you.

You are still there for me.
I am still here for you, Federico.

The Game of Patience

I play patience with myself.
It is life's slowest game.
This is the card with your face
staring up at me.

I turn it over,
and then I pray
that when I turn it again,
you will not have left me.

This is life's slowest game,
and I would
hesitate here
forever, slow-playing.

Star-Struck, Star-Crossed

We have had
such luck in our lives, Federico –
that night we drank together
until the dawn linked arms with us

in our stagger-walk homeward,
singing, laughing, dancing,
dictating to our crazy feet
which paths to take,

losing ourselves, and then finding,
one and then the other,
all that criss-cross patterning
of two star-struck, star-crossed lovers.

Baahling Federico!

You died for all the animals too –
pig, cow, rabbit, raven, sheep –
and they are refusing to eat
in homage to your passing.

Pig, cow, rabbit, raven, sheep
are standing in front of your grave,
asking: why oh why did they snatch him away?
What had he done to hurt them?

They croak, grunt, bellow, bleat:
He was our chronicler.
He lived inside our kingdom.
He was an animal like the rest of us,

Oh baaahling Federico!

The Wind Grieves for Federico

The wind will not walk away
from your grave today, Federico.
He has set up camp.
He has struck a note of defiance.
He will warn whoever comes to visit:
this man was the wind's man.
He was my goodness and all my future.
Through and through he understood me...

The wind will never cease
to remember you, Federico.
Your name will be in his least sigh,
his slightest breath,
his most furtive breeze
caressing the softest and slenderest of necks.
His hurricane griefs will be expressed
in the ripping up of trees,
and the deaths of, oh, so many.

He will tear, with a blind frenzy,
through all their lives
undiscriminatingly...
They will never hide from him, your killers.
The wind will prove to be
the most terrible,
the most merciless
of all your desperadoes,
my darling Federico.

Not Just Yet, Federico

Let me rest here for a little while longer
now that the darkness has
eased itself across me...

There will be little time enough for rest
when the light startles me awake
at day's call,

demanding that I speak for him
before the tribunals;
that I stand on street corners again,

bellowing forth his perjured name.
You have killed an innocent man!
I hear myself, with ringing clarity,

crying it out loud again.
My voice is shouting,
on and on and on...

No, no, no, no, not just yet, Federico,
spare me a little rest.
You would not want me to suffer for your sake.

You would wish to tuck me in here alone
and then tiptoe out to the landing,
with the candlestick in your hand,
flickering, faltering,
as the smile of you,
and the touch of your hand
fade from you.

Federico's Impatience

I have spoken of our two lives.
I have told of how I met you.
I have remarked upon your eagerness,
your fury,
and of how words, words, words
streamed from you.

Did I fling myself at you?
Those months we were together,
they still run on inside me
with a terrible passion –
your voice, your tender kisses,
your impatience
to be gone, it now seems.

Believing in Federico

Federico has never stopped
dancing for me.
Even when I sleep,
and he sleeps beside me,
he is still dancing,
and they are all still applauding him,
louder and ever louder the cheering.

Must it go on and on forever then?
It must! It must!
Federico is nothing less than
a constellation
of whirling, dancing stars
at which we should all
look up and marvel.

There is no limit to his energies.
He will be with us timelessly,
stretched here over us
in all his light streaming,
and forever here beside me.
We will never stop naming him.
We will never stop believing.

Setting Federico Free

I climbed, agile as a ship's monkey,
up, up, and onto
the edge of the catafalque
and there I wrenched off, in fury,
the lid of the coffin.

See! See! It is empty!
I shouted, triumphal.
I knew he would be elsewhere.
I knew his spirit would not tolerate
such confinement.

They disbelieved me.
They showed me the body.
They heaved it up
and threw it
across my shoulders.

I shrugged it off, quickly,
and set it running, running
into the fields and hedgerows,
amongst the butterflies, the sheep,

the brindled cows who stood
in a circle around him
in homage to
his blessed presence amongst them.

Que raro que me llame Federico!

Who gave this strange name FEDERICO to me?

Was it dropped outside the door
on the morning of my birth?

Did a shepherd whistle it,
polysyllabically,
in the mountains
as he was driving his sheep?

Did the well water arrange it
in a magical configuration
of fallen leaves?

How, how did this name FEDERICO
ever come to be?

(Mother, will you tell me?
Will you raise your fallen head,
dry your eyes, and speak aloud
the reason for my being me
and always me?
Little snake in the grass,
can you help my mother?
She is so lost now without me.)

Federico's Whisperings

It was a night of most bitter wakefulness.
You had stolen him away from me.
We had fought over his body.
You had cut it into such tiny pieces.

I gathered them all up and I ran with him,
and as I ran, I kept dropping
all these precious little parts of him –
that waving hand, that beating heart.

I watched the heart, still pulsing where it fell,
but I needed to run on
because you were still coming after me,
and I was repelling your bullets, every last one.

It was Federico himself, I know that now,
his precious parts, his most precious relics
which were protecting me from all danger.
I knew that this morning

as I have never known it before
because he has whispered it to me
on the breeze; and the grasses,
they have nodded their grave assent, unanimously.

Together, Federico

Are we haunting those
dark, twisty back streets
of the Albaicín again, Federico?
Are you seated there beside me,

legs drawn up,
backs to dark, cool wall,
knees pressed tight together
in a knobbly, pale line of four?

Are we still those children that we once were?
Of course we are!
Not a thing has gone.
Not a memory has been forgotten.

Oh, how I rejoice in such memories.
They are all that my life has become.
They engulf me.
They fill me to the brim, and spilling over!

It Is All Too Awful

Let us not speak of it now, Federico.
Let us both sit here, hand in hand,
drink our drinks, on and on,
until the evening sun sinks behind us,

and we disappear into laughter.
There is no other way for us to go on.
There is no other future before us.
Could you suggest one?

Or are you already asleep in my lap?
Is your hair ruffled? Are you snoring?
Must I gently carry you indoors,
tuck you in, and then leave you?

Never To Know

Life continues impossibly,
this soundless, fruitless life
which holds my foot to the ground
with a leaden weight.

I am so barren.
I am a tree stripped of its life,
dead and yet upright still,
a mere pretence, a shell.

Help me if you will.
And yet do not help me.
You have your own sorrows to bear.

You knew him too.
He sang for you
as much as he sang for me.

The sadness is
that I can
never know you.

An Unexpected Invitation to Paradise

Would you want me to ask you again
why you left so suddenly that morning,
as if something of such urgency
was compelling you to leave me?

I noticed no such look when you closed the door,
quietly, behind you, and with such stealth in fact
that I barely noticed you had left me.
I would have said, half-dreaming,
        that you were still beside me.

But no. It was not so. And it will not be so forever –
if forever must consist of those days which
began on that morning, and run on now forever...
Yes, you have left me, Federico.

And you have not said one word to me yet
of what exactly compelled you to leave me.
Had someone spoken a word to you *sotto voce*?
Had they invited you to paradise unexpectedly?

A Prayer for Federico

Federico, this is a prayer for you.
It is as much as I can give you.
There is no more left of me
to share with you.
I am a remnant of all that you knew.

Federico, this is a prayer for you,
and it begins:

dearly beloved,
songbird of the trees,
cantor of the sacred Andalusian soil,
cloud-surfing angel,
intercede for me
with Him
in whose presence you stand,
naked and freely given
(and far too soon robbed from me)...

Unpicking Death's Mystery

No, no, I did not die yesterday.
It was all a rumour,
despatched on the wind
to diminish me.

See how I stand here in front of you,
arms spread, teeth gleaming.

Watch my fingers when I sit
and play the piano for you.

Is that not how it has always been?

In every flower's breath
I am breathing with you.

See, see how my flitter
is in the butterfly's wing!

My passing anger with you
is in the low cloud's brooding
over the roof tops.

My happiness is in
the re-awakening of the sun.

I did not die yesterday.
Nor shall I die tomorrow.
The word DEATH is a mystery to me.

And you tell me there is a gun which can unpick it!

Death, There Is No Word For It

Death, there is no word for it.
It is only a flavour, a fleeting flavour.
Sometimes the wind carries it.
Sometimes it is on the finger's end,
death's fleeting flavour,
death's tireless beckoning.

Death, there is no word for it.
Love long since denounced it, saying:
I am the greater one, the one to be feared.
Death kept its silence,
knows what it knows,
sees what it sees:
love, prostrate on the balcony.

Death, there is no word for it.
Humbleness becomes us all.
To speak a little. To crawl a little.
To see a little further until
that which befalls befalls.

Death's Intimacy

Federico, are you awake yet?

I am awake. I am always awake.
Can you not hear me?

Federico, are you stirring yet?
Are you listening to the breeze?

I hear it all. It is passing through me.
My spirit is forever quickening.

Federico, when the breeze dies away,
and the silence returns, your absence engulfs me.

I am the voice of the silence.
I make the silence speak so eloquently.

Federico, when I walk now, down this street,
it is as if everything is falling away from me.

Let me bring them back to you then.
Let me say: welcome him! Be a friend to him again.

He is so, so afraid
of death's intimacy.

The Cold Corridors

The candle-light is dying, Federico.
I can barely see the outline
of your body on the bed any more.
Would you say one word to me
to re-assure me that you have not left me?

I can never leave you.
Did I not make that pledge?

The dancers have left the door ajar.
Cold winds are blowing at this unseasonal hour.
Will they return to resume all that rejoicing?

The hour of rejoicing is at an end.
The long aftermath is now upon us:
the fear of the neighbour, the fear of the friend
that you will no longer recognise.
You must learn to walk
the cold corridors of hatred.

For All Eternity, Federico

Dearest friend, were you alone when I met you?
No, no, you were never alone.
They flocked around you
like the birds of summer,
listening to your voice,
laughing at your jokes.
I suffered such jealousy.

And now, at last, I have you on my own.
They cannot reach you.
They cannot fawn on you
because you are hidden here inside me,
beating heart next to my beating heart,
or perhaps we two are as one,
and one heart is beating now for both of us...

I peer in at every moment,
but especially at these moments
of acute aloneness,
when I see you, talking to me,
seated beside me,
never wishing to stir from me.
Why would you stir from me
when I have settled you here, so complete?

And so, at last, I have you now,
for all eternity.

Papa Death

You must have heard me
whisper those words to you,
of how death is a healing balm,
of how death reduces everything
to tranquillity in the end.
Let papa death take me then!
It is all too much for me.

The brightness in the bars,
the bruising talk, the noise...
I have invited my feet
to step more peacefully.
I have said to my reluctant feet:
you lead me now.
It is all a little too much for me.

Time Unmakes Its Favours, Federico...

You must have noticed that,
how the camellias shed their petals
across the coffin lid that day
as we all walked behind it...

Dearest compadre,
it was for you we were processing
with all due solemnity that day,
and yet we did not know it.

And you too were shedding bitter tears
for yourself over the loss of all
that was still to be written.

You were unsaying then,
petal by falling petal,
all that you would not say.

All Of This May Be You

I walk these streets
in a profound sleep.
It is as much as I am fit for.
I am at a loss for any more.

My hand no longer grips.
My head shakes uncontrollably.
What is this grief
which always so consumes me?

I know where you live
deep beneath the earth.
And yet I do not know at all.
They have dispersed you.

Dust on a table top.
The wetness of a tear drop.
The merest scrap of paper.
All of this is you. Or it is not.

Swimming with Debussy

Tune your instrument again, Federico.
It is all so off key.
You are not yourself today.
Why go away in disgust
when I am still calling to you?

Debussy is thirsting to be played.
I want to hear you afloat on his waves,
to see the spreading of your fingers
as you swim with a greedy urgency.

Are you pulling away?
Is that you, that tininess on the horizon?
Are the storm clouds rasping their horns?
Is the entire orchestra raining down upon us
as I so patiently wait here for you?

The Bottles

The measure of our love for each other
is in this twisty briar which makes
my fingers bleed even as I squeeze it.

When I catch that blood on my tongue's tip,
I taste again the ruddy sweetness of your lips
that day I punched you for your foolishness.

That blood was an enthralling horror to both of us.
The blood of martyrs, you sobbed,
      the blood of flowers,
the blood of the sunset we watched dying together

as the bottles heaped ever higher.

Since Your Death, Federico

Since your death, Federico, we have all been dying.
Little by little, decrepitude has overtaken us –
limbs stiff and shrivelled,
long hours of blankness,
a terrible, engulfing tiredness.

Since your death, Federico, we have all been dying.
The trees are reduced to black, skeletal fingers.
The flowers pillow their heads on barren ground.
The clouds are throwing their shrouds over us.
All nature is bidding us goodbye.

Since your death, Federico, my neighbours
have all given up the ghost.
They lock their houses with a sigh.
They carry so little away with them.
They queue in silence for the opening up
       of the gates to the cemetery.

My Death for Yours, Federico?

You lied to me on that day
when you told me,
with characteristic playfulness,
that we would die together,
in each other's arms,
having loved to the uttermost,
having sucked down to the marrow
all of life's bounties.

Now you have cruelly torn yourself away
without a word to anyone.
You have walked off the stage
without so much as a strut,
a backward look or a sigh.
You have not explained to me
why you needed
to throw yourself away like this,
so hurriedly, so wantonly.

Do you have no feelings for me any more?
Do you not understand that I am left here,
helplessly scratching at these walls
like a frenzied cat?
Federico, is it to be tit for tat?
Would you really want that?

Federico Is Not Dead

I have turned my back on it.
I have slammed the door once and for all.
I have denounced all those witnesses as perjurers.

In short, I have not accepted the fact of his death.
There is no law which obliges me to accept it.
No tongue can convince me of the truth of it.

No sung lament will persuade me.
No tears will reach me.
No sighs of a mother will beckon me to sigh in my turn.

No memorial, no matter how upstanding,
    will overawe me.
No god will convince me that it is true.
The fact of his eternal beauty cannot be
    torn away from me.

Federico, stand here beside me. You tell them.

This Endless Waiting

Stop. Wait.
There is time enough today
for ease,
for all this pain to dissipate.

Stop. Wait.
It was so easy, your gait.
I walked in step with you.
We knew such precious togetherness.
We called it our fatedness.
Foolishly.

Stop. Wait.
Such cold has descended.
A knife at the throat.
Robbed of all breath.
Sunset.

This endless waiting –
for what though?
Death. *Death*.

Questions for Federico

Is there any measure of your usefulness to me?
Are you an implement to be wielded?
Or are you an adornment for the body?

Do I carry you around with me?
Or are you quite separate
in the way that a stone speaks from a road
as if it both knows and does not know?

Where exactly are you, Federico?
I would wield you as if you were something mighty.
I would wear you to prettify me.
I would carry you. I would whisper to you.

I would stare at you
as a man stares at a gate to be opened
onto a field, where he then walks freely,
leaving it swinging, helplessly..

Federico Falls Away From Himself

I am slowly falling away from myself
as water spills from a jug, steadily.
Soon I will be everywhere.
Soon I will be nothing but
the damp stain on your stair.

I am slowly falling away from myself.
My voice is being diced into slivers
by a blade of such acuity
that you will scarcely hear
the thinnest echos of my voice
in the words that you use.
Even when they are my words alone.
Even when they are the very words
that I taught you.

I am slowly falling away from myself,
tumbling as a mountain slow-tumbles
down towards the sea.
Do not try to mimic me.
There is a method in my slow-falling,
and it is not madness.
It is a force of nature.

Your Killers, Federico

There is no forgiveness to be meted out
like sweets from a twist of paper.
What they did was damnable, wrong.
They will suffer the pain of it forever.

There is no mercy to be meted out.
Their trudging will be endless,
down roads of an unforgiving hardness.
Their very names will bring on forgetfulness.

They will not enjoy love any more.
All life long, they will be preparing themselves
for that foregathering at the river.
They will stare deep into hell's mouth.

And hell will swallow them, forever.

You Will Be Transported, Federico

My cry came unto you.
It climbed the air
until it reached you.
I heard you listening.
I heard you whispering
words of comfort.

I could not see you there.
The golden gleam of the cupola
was all I knew of you,
with that gathering
of saints and angels
in a circle around you,

protecting you
from all human sight,
protecting you
from all human harm,
leaning forward, arms outstretched,
preparing to transport you.

Broken

It came at such an hour as this one –
a quick, brutal bludgeoning
to the back of the head,
a single shot,
a single thrust of the knife,
so random to us,
so keenly calculated elsewhere.

We were scarcely aware,
such was the fear
in the heart of every man.
The helplessness of a shirt flapping on a line.
The helplessness of a chicken,
strayed into the road,
quick switching its neck.

The helplessness of mothers
staring at those lists of names.
Reading. Falling. Broken.
Forever after broken.

Federico is Not There

Did I wave back to you
as you retreated from me?
I forget now. Such is memory.
I count the days that came after.
They are all that is left of me.

Did I take up your coat
and offer it as you reached the door?
Had that cold snap in the air
made me do it?
Or was it my merely wanting
to settle it across your shoulders?

Your shape in the air
is still in front of me.
You are there, smiling.
You are not there.
I go on looking.
I will never stop looking.

Oh, the futile ransacking of memory!

**Often You Were Barely There,
So Sunken Were You Inside Yourself**

Your fingers are resting, lightly,
on the edge of the keyboard.
Should they take flight?
You stand up, with a shrug,
and walk off into the night.

To leave just as I arrived –
that was a habit you had
in the bad old days.
Pretend not to remember them, Federico.
Taunt me again.

Were you alive again to taunt me,
I could even bring myself to forgive you.

Federico, Fire Fly

We had such chances
to shine for each other!
Glow worms.
Fire flies.
Festive lamps
in the olive grove at carnival...

We danced.
(Your clumsiness
was always forgiveable.)
You stumbled.
(We applauded you.)
You fell.
(We now mourn your forever).

Showing the Way

Everything has stopped now –
all talk,
all movement,
even the itching of palms.

The outstretched arm
of the traffic policeman
will stay rigid
for all eternity.

He is indicating,
with due solemnity,
the path to the graveyard.

Fools, Fools

Who has been fool enough
to spill such a gift as this man
of a thousand talents –
poet, dramatist, pianist, clown...

And yet that is what we have done.
We let you go one day.
We dealt with you carelessly.
We let you slip from our hands
in the olive grove.
Life had always been so carefree
until it turned gravely serious.

Who has been fool enough
to spill such a gift as this man
of a thousand talents –
poet, dramatist, pianist, clown...

Is it not we?

The Curiosity of the Universe

Our last opportunity
to dance is here, now,
and so we seize it,

linking arms
and spinning frenziedly
until we both fall down

in an untidy, giggling heap,
only to help each other up
and begin again...

because, when we fell,
the music had hesitated to move on –
the spheres' music, that is.

The entire universe had stopped
and stared at us,
and almost shed a tear.

All

Now that I am free to speak of you, Federico,
I find that there is nothing to be said
because no words could be adequate
to sum you up.

To be truthful, you are dead.
Would you not agree?
Are you not all starlight now, all music,
all sights beyond all seeing?

About the author

Michael Glover was born in Sheffield. He is currently Poetry Editor of the *Tablet* and a senior art critic and feature writer for the *Independent*. He has been a regular reviewer and commentator upon the world of poetry for the *Economist*, the *New Statesman* and the *Independent*. He has written about poetry in performance for the *Financial Times*. In 2009 he established *The Bow-Wow Shop* (www.bowwowshop.org.uk), a free-to-access, online poetry magazine which has been archived by the British Library.

What other poets and critics have said about Michael Glover's poetry:

'Much energy and brio' – Seamus Heaney, Nobel Prize in Literature, 1995

'Michael Glover's lines unspool gravely and efficiently with few commas – like waves that know they are on their way to someplace, but without making much fuss about it. They can be piercingly sad and hilariously wry, sometimes at the same time. Michael Glover is a major find.' – John Ashbery

'Michael Glover gives us, often dazzlingly, the poet as performer, conjuror, clown, operating with a playfulness which, whether putting forward arguments about language, reality or poetry itself, is artful and frequently highly enjoyable.' – Laurence Sail, *Stand*

'Enviably idiosyncratic and, for that reason, attractive' – Joseph Brodsky, Nobel Prize in Literature, 1987

'Michael Glover, journalist, critic and poet, writes with clarity, wit and, best of all, he makes sense of nonsense.' – Barry Fantoni, co-founder, *Private Eye*

www.ingramcontent.com/pod-product-compliance
Lightning Source LLC
Chambersburg PA
CBHW061804070526
44586CB00023B/2706